Her Soul
beneath the Bone

Her Soul
beneath the Bone

WOMEN'S POETRY ON
BREAST CANCER

Edited by Leatrice H. Lifshitz

Introduction by

Phyllis Hoge Thompson

Foreword by

Rose Kushner

UNIVERSITY OF ILLINOIS PRESS

URBANA AND CHICAGO

Manufactured in the United States of America
1   2   3   4   5   C   P   5   4   3   2   1

This book is printed on acid-free paper.

Library of Congress Cataloging-in-Publication Data

Her soul beneath the bone.

1. Breast—Cancer—Poetry.   2. Women—Diseases—
Poetry.   3. American Poetry—Women authors.
4. American poetry—20th century.   I. Lifshitz,
Leatrice, 1933–
PS595.B73H4   1988   811'.54'080356   88-1348
ISBN 0-252-01518-5 (cloth: alk. paper)
ISBN 0-252-06008-3 (paper: alk. paper)

Photo on p. 71 is of Deena Metzger, photo by Hella Hammid. Taken
from the original poster (Tree, P.O. Box 186, Topanga, CA 90290).

Some of the poems in this collection have been published previously:

"Cathay," Patricia Goedicke (*Prairie Schooner* [Winter 1987])

"In the Hospital," Patricia Goedicke (*Epoch;* rpt., *For the Four Corners* [1976])

"100,000 upon 100,000," Patricia Goedicke (*West Branch* [Nov. 7, 1980])

"One More Time," Patricia Goedicke (*Three Rivers Poetry Review;* rpt., *Crossing the Same River* [1980]; also rpt. *Suturing Words* [1987])

"That Was the Fruit of My Orchard," Patricia Goedicke (*Seneca Review;* rpt., *For the Four Corners* [1976])

"The Weeping Place," Darcy Gottlieb (*No Witness but Ourselves* [1973])

"The Most Thorough Study of Women Breast Cancer Patients in the World," Susan Hamilton (*Communiqué from the Free Zone* [1985])

"To Mother," Julie G. Landsman (*Milkweed Chronicle* [Winter 1985])

"Scars," Elizabeth Lincoln (*Poets* [1978])

"Before Surgery," Jeanne Lohmann (*Where the Field Goes* [1976])

"Healing," Deena Metzger (*Tree* [1981])

"I Am No Longer Afraid," Deena Metzger (*Tree* [1981])

"Cat for a Neutered Lady," Bettie Sellers (*Green River Review* [1980])

"Zodiac," Phyllis Thompson (*New America* [forthcoming])

"Slant," Lorraine Vernon (*West Coast Review* [1979])

To Ruthann, who said, "Do it,"
and Rose, who said, "Why not?"

To Marjorie, who was there at the beginning
and Susan, who almost saw its completion

And, of course, to my mother . . .

Contents

Foreword

When I opened the slim, buff envelope that held the manu-
script of *Her Soul beneath the Bone,* the first thought that
occurred to me was exactly the one asked as a question in
Phyllis Hoge Thompson's introduction: "Why should any-
one put together a collection of poetry and 'narratives' re-
lated only by a curiously, narrowly defined theme: Breast
cancer?"

Then, immediately, I knew I had an answer. Women who
endure the double whammy of facing a potentially fatal
disease and, usually, the loss of a precious breast are filled
with feelings they must somehow get out to others. Some
women take photographs and express these feelings through
the lenses of their cameras; some women are gifted with the
ability to translate their feelings into drawings, cartoons, and
paintings.

In *Her Soul beneath the Bone,* more than two dozen women
who have undergone treatment for breast cancer have used
collections of ordinary words—their writing—to describe
their deepest, most personal feelings in a most extraordinary
way.

All women diagnosed to have breast cancer are terrified.
And along with the terror, they—no, I must say *we*—are
furious. But our fury has no particular focus. Should we, as
Deena Metzger asks in "Healing," lash out at the political
and social problems around us that might have created a
place in our breasts where stray, mutant cells implanted
themselves and began their deadly progression? Should we
blame laboratory "bench" scientists because there is no way
to prevent breast cancer? What about the doctors who exam-
ined us year after year, felt those awful lumps and assured us
that they were "nothing"? Or should we attack the surgeons
whose knives actually severed our breasts from our bodies?

Of course, some women laugh—or seem to be trying to make themselves laugh—at the experience. In "Mammogram," Terry Kennedy chuckles about her X-ray machine and the technician who snaps a picture of the innards of her breast. Leatrice H. Lifshitz, the editor of *Her Soul beneath the Bone,* jokes in "Ma" that her mother should somehow have "fixed" the breast cancer. All of these women tell the reader about a secret corner of their lives.

And all of these women want to share this secret corner.

So the answer to Thompson's question may simply be that most women who develop breast cancer have a desperate need to share their feelings with others.

Of course, I am one of them. Without even knowing that the awful lump I found in June 1974 was cancer, I kept—and still keep—detailed written and, whenever possible, tape-recorded notes about every step of the long and tortuous road from "early detection" of the tumor to my "rehabilitation" via the miracle of plastic surgery.

Unlike Lifshitz, Thompson, and the women who contributed to *Her Soul beneath the Bone,* I am a nonfiction medical writer—not a poet who writes beautifully and knows about metaphors. I read *Her Soul beneath the Bone* from the point of view of a reporter with an assignment to see if the changes in the way breast cancer is now treated are reflected in women's perceptions of the disease. Does a woman who knows in advance that her breast is to be amputated react differently?

Let me explain.

Until about 1982, most of the "feelings" I received from women, in letters or by telephone, were anger, fury, and rage about their treatment. This was the way it was, because—quite literally—the standard operating procedure was the so-called one-stage procedure. A suspicious mass was biopsied, and if cancer was found, treatment—usually a radical mastectomy—followed immediately. During those barbaric, not-so-long-ago years, the manuscripts that filled my mailbox usually aimed bile and venom at surgeons who had promised a Band-Aid after a twenty-minute little operation . . . but who cut a precious breast off while a woman lay unconscious on the operating-room table.

The constant theme from women who had endured this practice was, invariably, that they had been "duped." In their writings, they described the belief that something horrible had been "put over" on them while they were asleep and helpless. One example of those years—etched in my memory—is an essay, *I Came in with Two,* that had been illustrated with drawings that pictured the operating room as the kind of torture chamber used during the Inquisition.

By 1982, the one-stage biopsy-radical mastectomy practice was no longer routine in the United States, and diagnosis of a breast mass and its treatment were separated by days, weeks, or even months. Women then had time to get second opinions on both the diagnosis and treatment alternatives and to become adjusted to the fact that they had breast cancer.

By 1988, fifteen states had enacted laws requiring doctors to tell women diagnosed to have breast cancer about alternatives to mastectomy. Times had changed, and as I read the pages of *Her Soul beneath the Bone,* I tried to guess which of the undated works were written during the Barbaric Era and which reflected women's feelings as informed patients.

But there were few clues.

The kind of agony Lea Lifshitz has collected and brought together is timeless, most probably eternal. Nevertheless, my guess is that most of the poems and narratives were written in the current Enlightened Era, because the rage is a subtle, underlying theme and does not seem to be directed toward any duping doctor. The anger is aimed at the breast cancer as a disease whose treatment requires tearing a woman's breast from her body.

I tried to read *Her Soul beneath the Bone* with a poet's eyes; I tried to think the way Phyllis Thompson did when she wrote that breast cancer is "a rich and natural mine for metaphor." Unfortunately, the only metaphor this nonfiction medical writer can think of is the war in Viet Nam, where the enemy could not be identified and where it was often necessary to destroy a village in order to save it.

Some of the works in *Her Soul beneath the Bone* are bitterly humorous; some are grim; a few are plaintive; all are intensely private. The writers' "Why me?" anger and rage about having breast cancer are summed up in short, compelling autobiographical poems and prose.

These talented women have bared all of our souls to us. Certainly, every doctor who ever examines or treats a woman must read this book.

ROSE KUSHNER
Executive Director
Breast Cancer Advisory Center

Preface

Growth. Tumor. Malignancy. Breast cancer. These are words that invade our deepest fears, inform our darkest nightmares. And then, for some of us, there is the transformation to ordinary, palpable fact—*the* lump, the lump in the breast belonging to me.

But, of course, breast cancer and mastectomy, though common, are not ordinary; though statistics, are not simple; and though facts, do not exist in isolation. Mastectomies happen to individual women, people whom we know— mothers, wives, sisters, daughters, neighbors, friends, and lovers. How do these women get up in the morning? Go to sleep at night? Where does the scar of a knife on softest flesh hide? And what about the fear, the face of death?

To read this anthology is not a painless experience. If it were, it would not be honest and would serve no useful purpose. This anthology is a wail—a long, sharp, piercing wail; but it is more. If it moans, it also hopes. If it screams, it also quietly reflects. If it questions, it also seeks solutions.

The challenge of breast cancer and mastectomy is the challenge of change—not the slowly evolving change that we associate with life, but the cataclysmic change that drops like a death sentence and forces us into being who we are not. This anthology derives its strength from that challenge and its possibilities. It derives its strength also from knowing that the fear has been met, openly—in the bedroom as well as the office and kitchen, in the garden—always on the edge of tomorrow. There is little despair and much love in these pages.

Silence encourages denial, trivialization, and ignorance. It helps no one—not the person who needs to share or the person who needs to know. Women have always shared. It has been a way to make vital connections and a way to survive.

I am reminded of the number problems that I tried to solve when I was in grade school. If 100,000 women get breast cancer for how many years, what will that mean? What that means, for each one of us, is what this book is about.

Introduction

PHYLLIS HOGE THOMPSON

The question needs to be addressed head-on: Why should
anyone put together a collection of poetry related only by
a curious and rather narrowly defined theme: breast cancer?
The subject is, after all, medical. Such a collection could just
as well be invited on Altzheimer's disease or SIDS or asthma.
Even more closely comparable might be AIDS, since, like
breast cancer, this malady is both sexually related and topical.

Such an anthology strikes a note at the very least peculiar.
Apart from its strictly literary merit, then, what *use* is it?
Who in particular would find appealing a book so bizarre in
its limits?

Peculiar but engaging.

I first encountered this collection when I myself was mid-
way through writing a poem which took as a point of depar-
ture a friend's prolonged dying of breast cancer. I did not
choose the material; by its intensity, the experience forced
me to write. Because my friend was a woman of immense
vitality and power, her illness actually took over the lives of
those who loved her, draining, dominating, and absorbing
their energies and affections.

And the poem—I found it impossible to overlook the
compelling metaphor of the disease which eats away from
within at the spirit and vital force housed in the body. As
Susan Sontag writes, "Two diseases have been spectacularly,
and similarly, encumbered by the trappings of metaphor: tu-
berculosis and cancer."[1] For strictly literary reasons, if I may
be so callous, breast cancer turned out to be something I
needed to write about. Cancer, the sidling crab of the zo-

---

1. Susan Sontag, *Illness as Metaphor* (New York: Farrar, Straus and
Giroux, 1977, 1978), p. 5.

diac: it brought to mind my friend's crabbiness during her long decline. Of course, there were periods of exultation as well as periods of peace, but the crabbiness was part of the cancer.

Because my friend's malady was specifically *breast* cancer, the cancer seemed to me a metaphor for love, which is said to reside in the heart, which is said to reside in the breast. I found that in writing about breast cancer I had found a theme whose associative complexity was unavoidable. In turning the pages of the manuscript of *Her Soul beneath the Bone,* therefore, I was not at all surprised to discover that others had happened on the same treasury as I had. Far from being outré, breast cancer as a theme seemed a rich and natural mine for metaphor, possibly almost *too* ready to hand, once it had occurred to a writer as an expressive device. In saying so, I speak with the unfeeling obduracy of the artist who has an eye to the main chance, and other writers represented by work in this volume found the same propriety and justness in the theme, this, despite Sontag's statement that "cancer is a rare and still scandalous subject for poetry." [2]

In "Breasts" Joanne Seltzer calls love "the worst malignancy we've / ever known." "Consultation" by Tess Enroth must, for its full effect, be taken metaphorically, though its epigraph directs the reader to think of cancer. Other poems also demand to be read in the same manner. In Terry Kennedy's "Mammogram" "the technician [who] lowers the boom / on your breast" gets his own back from the woman who remembers "swinging the world by its ballicky tail."

The collection is a vigorous and varied utterance, unsentimental, of a sober and realistic mode. The subject is treated intelligently, dispassionately, respectfully, wittily—never evasively. The women whose work appears here have written about breast cancer with honesty and without qualification or illusion.

2. Sontag, p. 20.

Therefore *Her Soul beneath the Bone* will engage those who are sufferers from this cancer and those who, one way or another, have recovered from it, as well as those others who treat them, those others who love them. That a spirited creative reaction to the experience is possible is itself heartening; and to the extent that such work invites responsive analysis of the condition or acknowledges the various kinds of deep feelings it elicits, the book is surely valuable. It is useful to comprehend, for instance, the possibility of loss or hope or embarrassment or fear or laughter evoked by mastectomy.

To express these kinds of feelings in an art form is especially important, insofar as art gives a more fully interpreted image of things as they are than autobiographical modes can offer. Art is better able to help us understand what goes on. Autobiographical narratives generally lack the clarity the artist achieves by distancing and shaping the material, for art originates in focus and clear seeing.

The poems demonstrate that such an individual life experience is not confined to a single individual nor limited to a single or to a physical meaning. Yet such experience in the instance of breast cancer *is* confined to women.[3] That fact is necessarily central to *Her Soul beneath the Bone*. And since breasts yield milk, they manifestly characterize womanliness in an obvious physical way. For a woman to contract cancer in the part of her body most closely associated with nourishing a child after birth is for her to be assaulted in the fulfillment of a major role. *Her Soul beneath the Bone* makes clear that a woman's response need not be the loss of her sense of womanliness, nor of her femininity either, despite any male fixation on the breasts as a mark of beauty.

Breast cancer brings out a whole realm of feelings about what being a woman means, and the poems in this collection address those feelings with intelligence, empathy, and art.

3. Although there may well be a quibble in that men also may contract this disease, *breast* certainly first of all calls up the image of a woman.

They do not present the final word, of course, but they are especially interesting in regard to the question of where a woman's femaleness resides. Her nourishing function and her sexual attractiveness rest in her whole being, not in her breasts alone, but the sense of loss and the need to confront changes which accompany mastectomy and lumpectomy are real for a woman, even when she is perfectly confident about her personal worth.

Her Soul beneath the Bone is therefore comforting as well as informative. The poetry treats honestly the feelings which are aroused in response to one particular disease uniquely female, but because that disease strikes the breasts and may hurt or destroy them without destroying the woman, the feelings regarding breast cancer are not limited to feelings about disease. They also involve self-image very deeply. Therefore this collection is widely varied and interesting in a way not likely to be characteristic of responses to any other sexually limited malady. Because the tone of the whole, moreover, is heartening and hopeful, the book may not only comfort and inform; it may even inspire. I think these are sufficient and admirable motives for a somewhat peculiar book.

Her Soul
beneath the Bone

Healing

DEENA METZGER

Cancer surprised me as it does everyone else. When it came,
I had to ask: What are the voices in me which say "Die," and
which are the voices which say "Live!" I asked, "What are
the contributing factors to the disease, the political, social
elements which create a cancerous environment for us to live
in? What are the personal elements which contributed to the
illness? What imbalances in my relationship to others and to
myself need to be altered?" To return to health, I had to
scrutinize my life, root out the destructive elements, be sur-
geon and seer to my own psyche, make the necessary changes
which the life demanded. I had to see the disease as metaphor,
interpret it, and act accordingly. So I changed my life, I
learned how to protect myself better from the lethal ele-
ments in the environment, I learned to distinguish the exter-
nal and internal enemies, to define all my allies. I mobilized
a healing community, and finally I used the imagination as a
major tool for healing.

In the Hospital

PATRICIA GOEDICKE

When they came at me with sharp knives
I put perfume under my nose,

When they knocked me out on the operating table
I dreamed I was flying

When they asked me embarrassing questions
I remembered the clouds in the sky,

When they were about to drown me
I floated

On their inquisitive glances I drifted
Like a leaf becalmed in a pool.

When they laid harsh hands on me
I thought of fireworks I had seen with you,

When they told me I was sick and might die
I left them and went away with you to where I live,

When they took off my right breast
I gave it to them.

One More Time

PATRICIA GOEDICKE

Next morning, at the Medical Center
Though the X-ray Room swallows me whole,

Though cold crackles in the corridors
I brace myself against it and then relax.

Lying there on the polished steel table
I step right out of my body,

Suspended in icy silence
I look at myself from far off
Calmly, I feel free

Even though I'm not, now
Or ever:

The metal teeth of Death bite
But spit me out

One more time:

When the technician says breathe
I breathe.

Mammogram

TERRY KENNEDY

you stretch on a table
wondering how you got into this cage
the room with the X-ray machine
the god-eye-ball test
(checking your soul). go ahead faint
no one will notice.
everyone locked in her own vague hell.

the technician lowers the boom
on your breast
and a picture clicks in your brain:
the day you spent strutting and laughing
swinging the world by its ballicky tail!

For Hatfield, the Radiologist

TERRY KENNEDY

for hatfield, the radiologist
who sends me
postcards from japan

it's really masculine, phil
reading women like a book the way you do
seeing through their breasts
into that pea-sized death
every woman knows she owns from birth.

if you ask me
i'll say it's something to think about.

your eyes, those two blue prophets,
peering past flesh
into the source of milk
uncovering the hours left.

all day you liberate mothers
or hand them back to god.

if you ask me, phil
i'll say it's something to figure out
as you sail around duxbury bay
or stand at a urinal in tokyo.

Mammogram

JOANNE SELTZER

Strip to the waist and put this on, leave it
open in front so the doctor can feel
for lumps . . . come along, lie on the table,
roll away from me, now toward me. Wait,

don't look down, grab your left breast,
squeeze it tight, tighter and higher, don't smile,
now take a shallow breath, stop, hold real
still, that's right, relax, OK . . . we'll do it

now on the other side . . . now we'll sit you
up to do it . . . keep your chin up, don't move,
you're doing fine, hang on to that breast, don't

you want to live forever? And why not?
Your spirit feels trapped in your body? Love
hurts like cancer? You've lost your soul, have you?

Diagnosis

JOAN HALPERIN

On the third of May
the blunt forefinger of a doctor
pokes at a tumor
he says is in my breast.
His voice turns the new grass yellow.

Sucks his bottom lip
Loads his camera with X-ray film

I can see dandelions from his window.

Later that week
I lift the winter covers
from the sofa and chair
and hose the summer screens

　　Grave in the softness once fresh with milk.
　　Where is the mother who once suckled me?

The wind blows softly.
I have lost a part.
A part.

I am a moth
ready to burrow in winter clothes
surrounded by white nuggets.
Camphorized.

Before Surgery

JEANNE LOHMANN

Tomorrow I go to the hospital.
Mother, I wish you were here.
The doctor calls the cutting
he will do
"modified" and "radical,"
twin words, a pair
that break on one another.
He's scheduled a bone scan.
My bones that formed in you,
my breast that they will take.
There's a connection
that I need to make again.

Men touch our breasts;
they say they "know" us,
but something slides away.
My husband cannot work.
He loves me,
he is afraid,
he cries.
I've asked our friends
to care for him.
Our daughters know.
I'm petrified.
I love my body,
and my life.

Tomorrow I go to the hospital.
Your death is a distance, Mother.
Come here, and hold me now.

Ma

LEATRICE H. LIFSHITZ

Ma, you should have fixed it
you know when they did it
and left me with dumb skin
instead of a breast.

You should have fixed it, Ma
kissed it and made it better
like a knee or elbow, a nipple
has a right.

Really, Ma, be honest
wasn't that a promise
that I am in your image
that you squeezed me from the night?

No knife can slice the moonlight
no milk can come from stone
Ma, you should have fixed it
you know when they did it

when they cut away your mask
and made us less.

To Mother

JULIE G. LANDSMAN

I can't imagine you with only one breast.

Remember,
    When I was eleven
    And the only time we could talk alone
    Was when you took your bath?
    I'd sit on the floor beside the square tub
    Rest my elbow on the cold porcelain.
    You'd lean back in the sudsy water
    And listen
    As I told you about Janet Willoughby
    How all the boys said
    She'd let them do anything with her
    Out in the field
    Behind Stoddard's unused chicken house.
    Sometimes
    I'd stare at your brown nipples.

Remember,
    When I was eighteen
    And we went to the beach for the entire day?
    I'd turn on warm sand
    Brown myself all over.
    You'd sit in a canvas-backed chair, reading.
    You'd pull sandwiches and iced tea out of the red plaid
        cooler,
Lean toward me.
    You had a deep line between your breasts.
    I wanted to be as full as you.

Remember,
    When I was twenty-four
    And you came to me after Aaron was born?
    You came to clean house
    Make meals
    Wax the kitchen floor.
    We watched as my son pulled streams of milk from
        each of my breasts.
    We listened to the humming from his throat.
    Before you left me
    In the middle of the Minnesota winter
    You held me.
    We stood on the icy sidewalk,
    Yellow cab waiting patiently, motor running.
    I felt your fullness then.

Last August
It was my turn to come to you.
I didn't hug you.
You couldn't lift your arms
To put them around my shoulders.

I came
To clean your house
Make meals
Wax your kitchen floor.
I sat in the sun
Above New England hills,
The sea was a chip of mica
In the distance.

I never saw you naked
Was careful
Not to come upon you

Suddenly
Didn't ask to see the empty place.

And now
You call.
You say you're healed.
You leave for England.
You can lift both arms
the next time we meet.

Recovery

EMILY SIMS

Midsummer sun
glares in your face
car horns record stores blare
why has your sister
brought you downtown
if not to the big department store?
why has she pulled you past it
down a side street
you have never seen?

downtown changes here
there are trees
a huge red-brick building
she takes you inside
it has supermarket doors
she tells you
you were born here

the lobby is gray
the desk is gray
the receptionist, elevator, corridor
are gray
and the light
in the dim green room.

Here your brothers and father
their arms looking too long
stand a distance from the bed.

A nurse bends over your mother
pumping air into her mouth
through a clear plastic tube.
A faint electric hum.
Your mother opens her eyes
looks at all of you
the tube still in her mouth.

Complications

EMILY SIMS

late evening
by the open window
in the kitchen
lit by one light

feel how summer
has almost passed

crickets quieter
than the first nights
of your mother's absence

dark, having arrived
hours ago
rests comfortably

the kitchen is spotless
by your handiwork
your brothers
still out playing ball
you stand in the quiet
wearing
your mother's nightgown

think of her
waiting
these five weeks
intensive care
staphylococcus

fighting inside her
your father
her husband
her only visitor
twice a day

the nightgown
no longer reaches the floor
but hangs
above your ankles

almost full-grown now
you stand
barefoot on the cool floor
sipping cocoa
like your mother
how she never sits
for her evening tea

he appears suddenly
looms shouting curses
you are a small replica of
his wife
you burn your tongue
at the interruption
slam your mug
down on the stove
scream up at him
I'm afraid, too, daddy.
Scared as hell.

Separation

MIRIAM R. KRASNO

Twice in ten months
a lump grew in your breast.
A surgeon carved out the swollen tissue.
The scars deepened in your body
with the closing, hardening of your heart
after he left you last summer.
For days you do not hold your daughter,
afraid she will nudge your pain.
When he takes her these weekends
your lips no longer press her forehead.

Your body is ripped apart, invaded
first by him, then her.
Now strangers take parts of you away.
Bit by bit
you disintegrate in pain
as your child watches.

Obsolete

CATHY MAYO

Laser with ruffled edges
from womb to breasts   more
sensual than any sex

curls of child sweat
one eye watching light motes on my face
the other asleep creased by my bra
graceless legs outgrown by torso
draped trusting down my lap
hand of smooth sticky dimples
linked to my teeth
sucking in waltz time
stale baby breath moving
an almost hairless breast

six times I lengthened
this longer than was proper
for sheer pleasure
hoping I could wet-nurse for a living
after I had borne all
allowed babes

they tell me now to start over
to learn
a flat-chested talent
and there is no time

Dedicated in memoriam to Phyllis Schmeeckle
who discovered her breast cancer while nursing
her sixth baby

[18]

Injunctions

JOAN HALPERIN

My mouth opens and closes around the word cancer.
Tell the ring finger that probes
that I will not be host another time.
The doctor that I believe and doubt his reassurances.
I have developed artist's fingers
that trace the contours of my breast.
Fingers of a plumber digging beneath granular tissue.

When did the sun turn white and start to wither
plants and ferns with such intensity?

Inform the husband that I do not want my life measured
        by time and obligations because I love.
Whisper to the children that I will hold them in my
        naked arms
and spread my knees wide enough to crawl between.
Ask them to wrap their arms around my neck.
Sing me a song of such clarity I will know
that this is only one of many Springs to come.

That Was the Fruit of My Orchard

PATRICIA GOEDICKE

No moon. No night
    Either.
        White as the inside of an onion

Bed after hospital bed stretches
    Endlessly to the sky.

In the shadowless country of loss
    Wafers of silence whirr,
        Knives like hummingbirds flicker,

Silently they insert the needles,
    The scalpel cuts across
        The entire melon gapes open

And they scoop it out with a spoon
    Silently they throw it
        Where?

I, who was not there, tell you
    That was no nightmare.

Now, even though the scar lies
    Hidden under the grass

Sodium pentothal still blooms
    Coldly, everything smells of ether

And everything keeps murmuring

Loss is an endless column, cry
    Without sound, mute
        Bird that has flown too high,

And that was the fruit of my orchard
    They plucked

That was the field of my body
    They trampled

I, who was not there, tell you
    That was no nightmare.

Once There Was a Woman

PATRICIA GOEDICKE

Once there was a town with two hills
Rising over the valley

Once there was an old-fashioned street
With balconies over every door

Once there were children in that street and each child
Had two crackers to eat

Once there were two nipples like chickadees
Perched on top of a tree

Once there were two yellow and blue flags flying
Like cheers over the schoolyard

And once there was a woman with one round breast
And one flat one

Once there was a woman with two tears
Of self-pity in each eye

Once there was a soldier with two legs,
A city with two leaders

Once there was a piano teacher with two hands
Like pigeons, treble and bass both

And once there was a woman with two little strawberries
Like daughters, now she has none

Once there was a house with many people
Living in it, now there are none.

The Lump

The Swelling

The Possibility of Cancer

Notes from the Oncology Clinic

JANA HARRIS

for Peti Taylor

I
(Joleen)

sitting
she watches
cinder block hallways
lined in half-lives,
patients
on aluminum tables
sedated, waiting
their turn
in the room marked
radiation   danger

wig-headed and ashen-skinned
two women talking beside her:
Clara, in the hospital
we made jokes
on prosthesis—he
pinned a corsage
over her heart, and pop
exploded her falsie—

while with a ruler
a white-coated oncologist
measures Joleen's neck lump,
doesn't look like the men
Ma warned me about, men
with knives
who'll go for your throat,
thinking

the other words
of her childhood: *Jo-
leen, you grow up'n
argue with your husband
he'll leave you, hon*
—that the worst threat
like a razor strap
held up to her—why
she wonders, no one said
Joleen, if you
don't talk back
the words'll turn
to cancer in your mouth

why no one told her
the worst betrayal is when
your own body
turns on you, not
the male radiologist
rushing to the washroom
trailed by yards
of X-ray film
while white-faced
white-hatted nurses
fill the silence
with their smiles

and two technicians
whisper by the water fountain,
the danger of radiation
on them, lingering
no one eager
to get on
with the business
of death

the business of the grunt-talking
boy in the hall, face
battered, hair dog-chewn,
an orderly sitting
on his wheelchair arm
gestures: a shave?
a cigarette? their laughter
drowning the other voices
sedated
as Joleen says from them,
I want to go home

wondering
what kind of a sign
it is that she can't
make a joke on death, a hex
to hold in front of her,
and in her notebook begins
a poem, my sick joke on death,
she calls it, repeating
the words like a mantra
waiting for the radiologist
to translate her X-ray film;
malignant, terminal, operable,
benign

II
Is It Cancer or a Coloring Book?
(Joleen's Sick Joke on Death)

another prescription
for valium,
Dr. Nazi yawns,
My God, there's
a lump
in your neck! He
hails a hospital
gurney with red
customized wheels and
the rear axle
jacked up. Blue
Shield or Blue
Cross, he demands
scooting her down the
basement rivers of
an oncology clinic,
orchestrating her
entire condition from
biopsies to surgery
after lighting her
up on the inside to
see where her body
went wrong. Then
with blue-green felt-tipped
Crayolas, he
draws on her lump
following the
paint-by-number
nuclear medicine
chart on the wall. Sure

you're not pregnant?
he asks poking
her bump, cancer's
so common in women
getting older and pregnant
these days. He
draws red stitch
marks on her throat,
don't worry
about scars, he says,
we'll have you
sewn up and ready
for a Cosmopolitan
younger man/older woman
affair in no time,
dontchaknow?

III
(Clara)

a month after chemotherapy
my hair fell out, but
Joleen doesn't hear her
above the pencil
noising across the page
writing the poem
to blot out the words
of the wig-headed women:

Clara, the Faith Healer
I told you about? passed
her hands over me
touched my one breast saying,

feel a cool breeze here?
charged me fifty dollars,
and better make it out to cash
she says

eye lights burning
one nodding to the other,
Clara, I held it together
til the end, til I had to
sign my breast away
and now when I drink
cool water
instead of going
straight
to my stomach
it's as if it curves
filling up the hole
—phantom nerves, they say

eventually it goes away

Woman's Barter

TAMMY MAE CHAPMAN

The doctor gave her
what would help her improve:
    a fist-sized ball to
            clutch and release
            clutch and release
    after taking from her
    a part of herself
      her breast.

When brought to her
she would not touch this
            breast-ball—
            sexual stranger to virgin,
            hateful lover to partner.
She heard the voice of her girlhood preference
when asked to play in the neighborhood:
"I don't wanna play ball,
I wanna dress up like pretty grown-up ladies."

They gave her back her breast
            transformed
      into this ball
            waiting patiently,
            playing into her hands
      till she took it up
      as a weapon
      against loss

      breast with concave nipple
      something of her own
        to hold.

Consultation

TESS ENROTH

It is almost a rule:
breast cancer does not hurt.
—Bryan N. Brooke, *Understanding Cancer,* 1973

Try now to locate the pain.
Describe its nature,
intensity, duration.
We can, you know, alleviate,
sometimes can eradicate
                              what is
essentially a symptom.
Pain can't tell us
                         everything
Grave and mortal ills
often do not hurt.
But pain can tell us
                         something.
It may, like a baby's cry, mean
                         anything.
Try now to tell us
where and when the pain is most severe;
—Inside in darkness and alone—
tell us
                         nothing.

Post Mastectomy—Week One

MARIAN S. IRWIN

The hard new path
I follow curves from sight
beyond the hollow
of my heart.

My fingers,
kin to even this terrain,
are restless wanderers:
here there is pain, here pull,
and here, sensation gone,
I am my own unknown.

Unsure of where I am
I weep the loss
and wait
whatever certainty remains.

Now Only One of Us Remains

PATRICIA GOEDICKE

Now that the wave has come and gone
               Where are my feelings

Now that the sky has darkened and then lightened
               Where are my feelings

Looking at myself in the mirror who is it,
Who is that lopsided stranger
Washing up and down the shore

Now I have lost my right arm
               Where are my feelings

Heart flounders in the surf,
The crabs have it but where is it,

Now I am standing on a beach high and dry
               Looking for my feelings

Now only one of us remains
               Where are my feelings

Slant

LORRAINE VERNON

when a woman has
a breast removed
it seems The Other
becomes twice as precious

I look at myself now
In the mirror
Like a one-eyed
Goddess, or a painting
in a European gallery:
Not a romantic
But a surreal

Perhaps I am—
A Viennese maiden
with a single bosom
a statue eaten
by the water
of a faulty fountain
(eroded) or broken
by little boys
(who throw stones)

Or maybe I'm becoming
(androgynous)
precocious female—
child woman man
transforming Woman
with the little

(left

Does It Eat Too?

ZONA GALE

Anne's first night out
in full prosthesis
salad drops down front
laughter dissolves us
almost to tears
tension eases
after months of fear

Cancer in the Breast

PAT GRAY

is hard as the pit of a ripe peach.
Those who have it know it,
no matter what they're told.
Even the surgeon who puts you to sleep
knows you will wake up robbed.
(When he presses your breast,
it dimples toward its pit—a sure sign.
But this simple fact, he hides from you—
a black ace flickering in his sleeve.)

You dream a peasant lover,
a bold Serb,
vandalizing your thighs,
mowing the damp crop,
Plowman of the Dark Ages,
harrowing your breasts.
When you wake, one is missing:
this slash, his sign.

The glob of breast gone,
love becomes lopsided—
your husband's brave insouciance, new,
his kindness forming
a small pellet of distaste.
Finally, you can look at the scar:
a fierce horizontal slash
rounding your chest to the arm—
puckered and red as a rapist's mouth.

Even as death will never leave,
you breathe submission and hope,
a slanderous light by your shoulder.
You go in search . . . a peasant shape . . .
Under the green-splotched leaves
ciderous apples leak
an overripe sweetness,
and on your girlish legs,
a thin brown stain appears.

elegy

F. M. BANCROFT

1
severed
your breast
nipple upward
alone
out of reach
floating
in gray space

2
pulpy tissue
measured
weighed
fifty samples sliced out
archived "forever" in clear fluid

the softness could not be preserved

3
"I'm crippled," you said.
"My body is deformed.
It's hard to get used to.
Every day it looks worse."

4
The scar snakes hard
across the hollowed plain.
I thought you'd look like a man.
The crevice between your breasts is gone.
I miss having two to hold.

My fingers knead the survivor like a baby.

Mastectomy

KATRINA L. MIDDLETON

for Marie Butler, in memoriam

Sterile gloved fingers sliced
away my breast. Wrinkled
and sagged. No lover's fruit.
Not for twenty years now.
But, Doctor, it was mine.
Why couldn't you erase
the alien growth with
those fancy silver tools
yet leave the flesh? Piece by
piece. In seventy years
three daughters grown and my
husband dead. Piece by piece
alone. Now draped in white,
to hide black crosshatched threads,
I'm left with one more scar.

Mastectomy

KAY SCHODEK

Ptolemy.
The mummy retains his flesh
but I'm
twice robbed:
first of the hand
that caressed the breast.

The Nile continues
to curve around the pyramids.
My terrain's dry
and flat as baked clay.

Mastectomy

ALICE J. DAVIS

No cushion
muffles
my heartbeat—
skin pulled
tight as a drum

After Surgery

ALICE J. DAVIS

I am lopsided
flatter than a boy.
S-shaped stitches
frame washboard ribs.
Why should I remember
after seven years
the way a hand
curved my breast?
Old griefs sift through
this excavation.

I Must Explain

JOAN HALPERIN

why it is that
at night
in my own house
I watch for stars
that fade into the atmosphere
like specks of white wool
into the shabby wool
of an army blanket.

I cover the mutilation
of my breast with both my arms
and look upward from the corner
of the couch.
It is almost April.

You carry me to the bed,
the stove,
the heat of the fire.
I see your face flushed
with purpose.

My world tilts
Hailstones pound upon the roof.

An airplane,
its ten miniature windows lit
like a doll's house
passes overhead.

I can feel your warm thigh
with my cold toes.

You never shudder at my scar
and I am touching your hair.
I begin to weave
patterns
thoughts
strands of wool.

Cathay

PATRICIA GOEDICKE

(For Margaret Fox Schmidt, 1928–78)

Even after the chemotherapy I said O you,
Perfect roundness of celestial fruit
I'm nuts about you!

Your cupcake face sits
In the middle of the gold star of your hair
Like a child's picture of the sun smiling,

You fly over our heads such a bright snappy flag
Fuzzy with peach bloom but crisp,
Jaunty as a pirate,

What's in your hold is a mystery,
But cutting through the deep blue seas of your eyes
The tart juices spurt up, delicious

As candied ginger from Cathay,
And I'd load you into my market basket
Any day: there you'd roll around

Like a pale yellow melon rubbing cheeks
With lesser creatures: dull turnips, potatoes,
For you're not only the cream, you're the citrus in my cargo,

Just listening to you tell stories makes me jump up,
Hearing about all those swashbuckling ladies,
Your heroic chuckle like the rough chunk of waves

Keeps slapping at my sides with such encouraging spanks
I just wanted to tell you, for a Kewpie doll you're some dame,
For a gun moll you're some sweet seagoing daisy:

With your round face waving to me from the bridge
If just being around you for two minutes turns me into a
    fruitcake
All dippy and dizzy and brave as a gangster bee

Even with only one wing and a broken leg
All you'd have to do is say *Vamonos*
And I'd follow you anywhere, honey.

Elizabeth

LORENE ERICKSON

Most of all, he said,
he loved her breasts

praised with the sweet
let of milk.

He saw her, all,
but so much less.

> Emerald walnuts
> dry, turn black,
> in season fall away
>
> to razored ridge.
> Split one open—
> take the dearest meat.

She wished for such ripening,
or fire, swift

conflagration to burn away
her easy flowers

accident, to offer up
her soul beneath the bone.

In dream afraid
she called up salt

enough to poison rue
and her soft loam

gathered into pebbles
rocked upward

lodged stone
in the paths he remembered.

The mutilating blade
retreated, across her chest

a string of sutured pearls,
her gift for clarity.

He saw her, ruined;
never the grieved heart—salt.

Jonesie

ZONA GALE

Yes I'm fine now
two years
no flare-ups
check-ups normal
radical
radiation
chemotherapy
scary
worth it

I love my sales job
at the gift shoppe
meeting tourists
bosses like my work

home different
he hasn't touched me
since surgery
refuses to discuss it
or counseling

Cat for a Neutered Lady

BETTIE SELLERS

Her father loved cats, collected strays—
one big tiger tom who waited on the sideboard,
spat at her when she came for knives and forks

to lay the long oak table. Once she tried
to bathe him—and one leap sank ten claws
leaving crescent scars tattooed on her back.

She married a man who hated cats,
gave her babies who filled small
coffins like so many waxen dolls.

When he left her for a nursing home,
helpless as one of her dying children,
she went every day but never told

his crumpled face about the cat somebody
gave her. "He'd think I didn't want
him to come home," she said.

Now he sprawls his length across her breastless
gown, purrs like the rales of her chemotherapied
lungs. Neutered as he, she strokes his arching

back, ruffles her own scant fur. "It'll grow back,"
she claims as he hops down to bat an empty pill
bottle, dry plastic sounds across the bedroom floor.

She wears a wig when she goes out.

radical

GAYLE ELEN HARVEY

fear trembling, fire-dry, in pill-sheathed
darkness, wrenching me from sleep to bargain, one last time,
with those dwarf anarchists beneath my breast.
testing positive, this time tomorrow, I will lie lopsided,
pruned of those cells winking in my flesh
like hot, demented diamonds.

black-stitched, waiting for my husband's hand,
I shall be chastely sponged,
with one less secret, as we simulate our passion,
as we both pretend night hides my plundered heaviness,
this map of battle.

After Radical Surgery

SUE SANIEL ELKIND

In this twilight
before dawn
I drift sleepless
the budding of those slopes,
the times your hands, like a sculptor's,
played over those taut mounds
that were the key to my senses.
Now I am a dredged, dead sea.

These amputations repel.
We are two ex-lovers unstuck,
unmendable.
I will not lie here
wait for your love
while barnacles fix to my body.

Kaiser Hospital Trilogy:

Three Women at the Mercy

of Unknown Gods

SUSAN EFROS

I

a woman is slicing meat;
her thumb interrupts the chore.
wrapped in paper towels
she is driven to the emergency
door, where a 3 × 5 index
card greets her: "The emergency
room has been moved."
a trail of blood leads her across
the street, around a corner,
thru a corridor and into the laps
of doctors sipping coffee.
"We'll be with you in a moment,"
they say to the thumb, finishing
a private joke before putting
the needle thru her carelessness.

II

a second woman arrives open
flipped thru doors her body
concentrates on breathing life
between her thighs, works at
controlling pain, pushing
a labor of love.
they strap her to the table,
the slab they've known for an hour

and shoot her up with sleep.
her gift is lifted smoothly
from the ditch and a steady
scissors comes down to cut
the cord; a newborn child
swiftly wrapped and sealed away
from germs while the mother dreams
of giving birth.

III
a third woman receives foreign
signals thru her breast.
"a harmless cyst," the doctor
smiles. "you are a worrywart,
my dear." weeks later, the harmless
cyst is twice its size and bleeds
for an incision. the woman changes
color as rage pounds her chest.
unalarmed, the doctor concedes
to cut her open; the malignancy
flows out howling and will not stop.
two months later, the woman of 25
dies quietly at home; her lover
cradles her last bits of life
in his arms and dreams of mercy
from unknown gods.

Breasts

JOANNE SELTZER

I've two of them still, but if I had one—
or none—I'd love you as passionately
as I do now. What's a breast? Illusion.
An object for sending milk to babies.
And love? Love's the worst malignancy we've
ever known. Why should my nipples point up
at you? Nipples aren't created for love—
don't go crazy over nipples—don't grope
for something unattainable. There's no milk
left in me, and milk will never return
to me. I understand your need for milk—
no other food replaces milk—you burn
up for milk. This is the way of mammals:
we suck and we suck and we don't feel full.

Zodiac

PHYLLIS HOGE THOMPSON

In Memory of Vivian Milford
April 20, 1931 – April 20, 1985

The Sun's in Cancer when the woman comes
   To the river, seeking a place apart,
Feeling unsafe. The purple-hooded blooms
   Massed there flower beneath her heart—
     Bane of the Zenith by the flood
     Where she stands barefoot in the mud.
Love, the killing sugar, skims her blood.

While Autumn Sun rounds to the Equinox,
   Pink-lipped blisters kiss her bone
In secret. Wrapped in her hardy soul, she mocks
   The dimpling flesh. Yet, spent and alone
     In the night, she tosses, shiny-eyed,
     Wakeful with fear the omens lied.
The delicate, swollen blossoms sob inside.

She rubs the palpable matter in her breast.
   It grows familiar as the way
She sees herself. Her breath feels cramping, pressed
   From her lungs in sighs. The shortest day
     Leans upon Capricorn, embracing pain
     As it straddles her ribs, swathes her brain,
Then slips to her liver where soft death has lain.

Has labored all this while. Aching to go,
   She aches to stay. She wades in lies,
Weeping, "Heal me with love, however slow

The cure." But as the hours rise
  Around her bones with streams of peace,
  She smiles. She sees the Light increase
Till Night and Day become one pulse. And cease.

Not All Women Are the Same

DOLORES ROSENBLUM

Not all women are the same,
though each looks in the mirror of the other's face
and smiles, and looks away,
though in the end there's the mastectomy,
the skin like blotting paper, and hair like wire
while everything else softens and lets loose,
though there is always a white curtain
drawn over the surgical sun, and a table wiped clean
for hands to knot, tangled with rings,
and fine powder like ashes drifts from
the cracked china forehead rising
as the hair recedes,
though it should finally come unplugged,
a black O in a rubble of white linen,
not all women sit with their death daily
in rooms flooded with light.

Midnight

LEATRICE H. LIFSHITZ

Marjorie, it is midnight
the ancient time of women
and I carry you in my belly
like a baby that is growing
pink and healthy

It is midnight, Marjorie
and we are joined blood to blood
dream to dream, sacred sisters
as we plan to seed our gardens
and live

Marjorie, it is midnight
the magic hinge of time
and I am the moon
your mother, sister, friend
and in the custom of my people

I give you a new name:
it is dawn, it is morning
it is today and tomorrow
it is promise and spring
it is roses and apples

it is life
it is death to cancer cells

Marjorie, it is midnight
and I have named you

100,000 upon 100,000

PATRICIA GOEDICKE

Thinking of my friend Florence who teaches yoga (1)
Then of my friend Blanche the choreographer (2)

Also of my mother who died of it (3)
And of myself (4)

Then of my best friend Pat (5)
And of my friend Mary who died of it (6)

Then of my new friend Carole the actress (7)
And of my friend Catherine the musician who died of it (8)

Also the president's wife (9)
And the vice-president's (10)

And my sister Helen the schoolteacher who died of it (11)

Not to mention the hundreds and thousands of others
I know and don't know

How can I help it?
I think we are all cannon fodder,
Modern sacrifices, virgins

For the sake of the City's security
But above all for the sake of its wealth

Thrown to the monsters outside the City walls.

Sitting in the heart of the war zone
Among the embattled factories I see them:

Great companies of diseased cells
Looming on every horizon,

Grouping and regrouping, under cover
They are invading everyone:

Underneath the smoke, multiplying
Millions of tiny fibers

They are chewing each other up, they are breeding
They are turning themselves into real live animals,

They are stealing away all the wives!

One by one we are taken to the hospitals
In silence, in secret
The surgeons whet their knives

They are throwing us to the new dragon,
The one with a thousand eyes.

The Most Thorough Study of Women Breast Cancer Patients in the World

SUSAN HAMILTON

500 women in Italy
who had breasts cut off
because of malignancy
survived
in greater numbers
than women elsewhere
that have been similarly documented.
The doctor surmises
this high survival rate
is due to the relatively high dosages
of 5 FU, Methotrexate, and Cytoxan.
The study in Italy
continued for 5 years
but didn't go
beyond that.

Healing Dance

PATRICIA JAMES

I.

Before me you lie healing.
I give you my serene face.
We will dwell this year in the
Land of the Fathers, and listen
while your pain echoes
in some tomb of my memory.

II.

Mirror, mirror your
face, mirror your limbs
mirror, bruises mirror organs
on a surgeon's tray
mirror
victim
mirror: this
is how they do our lives.

A voice stabs dull like an old ice pick.
It's yours, throbbing in me the dull
pain of your chanting
mirror   victim   this is how

Lead-eyed mirror I pick
up the chant, echo a
beat behind, dance
into numbness   you lead. We covet
our guilty secrets:
this is how we do our lies.

Dwelling in this place, rage
gone cold, skin hardens.
At absolute zero we come frozen
into silence:
  we don't chant
  we don't dance.
Gaze upon the totem of our fears:
The Father's angry faces are
but dead and frozen wood.

With fever I am visionary
and my skin hurts
  sounds hurt
  thoughts hurt
the thought of you hurts,
of me (this is how they did our lives)

I see trails blazed by molten blisters
where I will dance and
the air crackles with your chant.
We burn their angry faces at their stake,
cleanse our lies.

The Weeping Place

DARCY GOTTLIEB

Her self
        lost to herself
she has gone
to confront the high
priestess, Necessitas.

                        There
in that distant
weeping place laired
        with unspeakable sorrow
she will battle
the lustful bruise, waiting
to snare her with pity—struggle
in the red darkness.

                        Alone
ferry herself across
the mirrored chasm.

She will lie
        in her own shadow
a seedling waiting to stir

                        learning
what she already knows: how change
risks growth, pain springs wisdom.

Poem for the Woman

Who Filled a Prosthesis

with Birdseed, and Others

SALLY ALLEN MCNALL

when I weaned my girl,
my last baby,
I kept crying the whole time
my breasts dried up—
for days I dripped
milk, tears, milk, tears—
dreamed I was
a bottle, the kind
that collapses,
inside a stiff, white frame

two weeks after they cut
off your breast
I woke up saying
"in a modified raspberry
garden"
modified—that means
they didn't cut out
arm muscle, means
when you don't hurt
you'll hug me
as hard as ever,
and your daughters

my mother's new breast
cost more than $100 and the girl
at I. Magnin's was so
matter of fact "you'd
think
everyone was doing this,
after all I never *did*
think
of myself as
an Amazon,
it feels quite real, feel"
—I'd felt the
scar, already, for fever—

we burn, we leak, we ooze blood,
tears, words, ink, milk

your decoupage
Mary's white side
feeding baby Jesus
Jesus' red side
is a good joke

we have got something off
our backs, too,
to balance us

do men
who feel something growing inside,
or suddenly piss blood
get more scared
than we do?
what do you think?

we're not Amazons,
the war's in
another place
we're ripe gardens now
red bumpy berries
full of seeds

hold tight,
there's no shield
anywhere
it feels quite real, feel

hold me,
our little girls
the bumpy earth
simply soak the earth
the air
the page

Scars

ELIZABETH LINCOLN

There's a white crooked scar
at the bend of my left thumb,
the rope-burn the spinnaker made
the only day I ever knew Jeff,
the day we all sailed down
the West Passage singing,
for the last time, singing.

Under my blouse, over my heart,
a ridge of scar
molds on a field of bone.
I can trace the motions
of the surgeon's knife,
its dull and futile dance
over my soft, dissembling skin.
I try to master it with art.

But this little mound
I made on my thumb
just before Jeff drowned,
that is the unnecessary wound,
the cosmic one, the one
I can't conquer.

So vast, so bewildering
the jagged edges we live on.

A Single Pearl

JOAN HALPERIN

lies on the black table.
No one can place a finger on the pearl.
The pearl repels touch.
In the grey shadows of the sky
the pearl's image floats
detaches from the mass
floats toward earth.
The pearl fills cavities
enters voids.
The pearl seeds the barren places.

As I stare out the window
the winter trees are barren and brown in the dusk.
I rub my fingers across my flat chest
next to the remaining fullness.

The pearl drops like a tear
allows me to mourn and caress both sides.
The barren trees become my consolation.

Clouds shift in the darkening sky
retreat into dark
and the solitary pearl on the table of glass
is pulled toward the heart of the moon.

I Am No Longer Afraid

DEENA METZGER

I am no longer afraid of mirrors where I see the sign of the
 amazon, the one who shoots arrows.
There was a fine red line across my chest where a knife
 entered, but now
a branch winds about the scar and travels from arm to heart.
Green leaves cover the branch, grapes hang there and a bird
 appears.
What grows in me now is vital and does not cause me harm.
 I think the bird is singing.
I have relinquished some of the scars.
I have designed my chest with the care given to an illumi-
 nated manuscript.
I am no longer ashamed to make love. Love is a battle I
 can win.
I have the body of a warrior who does not kill or wound.
On the book of my body, I have permanently inscribed a tree.

Contributors

F. M. B A N C R O F T is an editor and writer. Much of her work has been with educational and computer material.

T A M M Y M A E C H A P M A N ' S work has appeared in several poetry journals. She won first place in a national poetry competition sponsored by Brigadoon Publications.

A L I C E J. D A V I S was a social worker. Her poems were published in journals such as *Dark Horse* and *The Christian Science Monitor*. She died of cancer in 1985.

S U E S A N I E L E L K I N D has been widely published in poetry journals such as *The Panhandler, Kansas Quarterly, Beloit, Louisville Review,* and *Kalliope.*

T E S S E N R O T H has been published in poetry journals and is now working on fiction. She writes, "It has been almost fourteen years since my mastectomy and almost that many since I heard my husband's cruel rejection, believed him, and left. Now I am getting ready for a summer in Paris and Turkey . . ."

L O R E N E E R I C K S O N teaches writing and literature at Washtenaw Community College in Ann Arbor, Michigan. Her poetry appears in the anthology *Woman Poet: The Midwest,* edited by Carolyn Kizer, and in journals such as *Passages North* and *Green River Review.* Her first book of poetry, *Seasons of Small Purpose,* was published by Grand River Press. She was awarded first prize in the Judith Siegel Pearson national competition for a body of work on themes relating to women.

Z O N A G A L E has work published in poetry journals such as the *New Kent Quarterly.* She also reviews books for *Motheroot Journal.*

P A T R I C I A G O E D I C K E has published eight books of poetry; the most recent are *The Wind of Our Going* and *Lis-*

ten, Love. Her work has appeared in numerous journals and anthologies, and she has given readings at colleges and institutions including the Library of Congress, the San Francisco Poetry Center, and the YMHA Poetry Center in New York. She is currently an associate professor of English at the University of Montana in Missoula.

D A R C Y G O T T L I E B has published in numerous poetry journals and won the Dylan Thomas and Christopher Morley awards. She has read at the Folger Shakespeare Library and the Library of Congress. She has given workshops at The Womanschool, the International Women's Writing Guild, and at Green Haven Correctional Facilities. She has taught at the University of Miami and the State University of New York at New Paltz. She is the author of *No Witness but Ourselves* and *Matters of Contention.*

P A T G R A Y is a freelance writer for *WORLD* magazine, published for children by National Geographic. She is a member of the Poetry Society of America, has published in literary magazines, and works full-time for the Library of Congress.

J O A N H A L P E R I N is a teacher and therapist. Her work has appeared in poetry journals such as *Pudding, Poet Lore, Broken Streets,* and *Blue Unicorn.*

S U S A N H A M I L T O N supports Cincinnati's Center for Peace Education, where she worked as a volunteer, and is a member of SANE, WAND, and WILPF. She received an M.A. in English from the University of Cincinnati, specializing in twentieth-century American literature.

J A N A H A R R I S has published five books of poetry, including *Manhattan as a Second Language,* and one novel, *Alaska.* Her poetry has appeared in *Ms., The Nation, New Letters,* and the *Ontario Review,* among others. For six years she was director of the literary series of the Manhattan Theatre Club, Writers in Performance. Presently she teaches creative writing at the University of Washington.

GAYLE ELEN HARVEY has been nominated twice for a Pushcart Prize, won first prize in the American Poetry Association's "Words of Praise" poetry contest, and placed fifth in a *Writer's Digest* poetry contest. Her work appears in poetry journals such as *Mississippi Review, Hanging Loose, Xanadu, Nimrod, Stone Country, The Christian Science Monitor,* and *Plainsong.*

MARIAN S. IRWIN has published a book of poems, *Boundaries.*

PATRICIA JAMES is a trainer for several domestic violence agencies and teaches self-defense to women and children. "The Healing Dance" was written for a friend after her surgery.

TERRY KENNEDY was the recipient of a Fels Award and a Fulbright Fellowship. She was a MacDowell Colony Fellow and was nominated for the Pulitzer Prize in poetry. She is the author of five books of poetry and has published in journals such as *New York Quarterly, Massachusetts Review, Chelsea, Carolina Quarterly, Denver Quarterly,* and *Boundary II;* also in *Ms.* and *Sojourner.* She is the editor of *Red Radiator Rag,* an anthology of women's poetry, and of the Feminist Writers' Guild Newsletter. She is interested in translating the work of contemporary Polish women writers.

MIRIAM R. KRASNO is a Chicago–based writer and editor, and an active feminist. This is her first published poem.

JULIE G. LANDSMAN has published in literary magazines such as *Milkweed Chronicle, Sing Heavenly Muse!* and *Passages North.* She is a facilitator in a program for behavior problem students in Minneapolis Public Schools and is a teacher at The Loft, a Minneapolis organization for writers.

LEATRICE H. LIFSHITZ has been published in poetry journals and anthologies. She was a resident at Blue Mountain Center and has won several poetry awards and prizes. She was a founder of Rockland Poets and of the

Rockland County Haiku Society, which sponsors the annual Loke Hilikimani Haiku Contest. Presently she is working on an anthology about old women.

ELIZABETH LINCOLN had a mastectomy in 1973 and two recurrences since then. She attended Dr. Bernie Siegel's ECaP (Exceptional Cancer Patient) groups. Her poems have appeared in *Poets, Sojourner, The Other Side,* the *Providence Journal,* and the *Northeast Journal,* among others. She has published a book of poems, *Momentary Stays,* and *Tracing Shadows,* a biography of her great-grandmother.

JEANNE A. LOHMANN has published three books of poetry, most recently *Steadying The Landscape.* New work is current or forthcoming in *America, Blue Unicorn, Buffalo Spree, Crosscurrents, Plains Poetry Journal,* and *Yankee,* among others.

CATHY MAYO has been writing and publishing poems for the past seven years. She attended the Bread Loaf Writers' Conference in the summer of 1986. She works for the Office of Continuing Education at Vermont College of Norwich University.

SALLY ALLEN MCNALL teaches at the University of Kansas. She worked on *Images of Aging,* an oral-history-into-poetry project and publication of the Lawrence Arts Center. She held a teaching Fulbright to New Zealand in 1983. She has published in *New Letters, Cottonwood, Cape Rock, Anima, Spoon River Quarterly, Womanspirit, Kansas Women Poets, Confluence, A to Z, Plainswoman, Red Cedar Review, Kansas Quarterly,* and elsewhere.

DEENA METZGER is a writer who has been leading writing and journal workshops for twenty years. She developed *Healing Stories* as a therapeutic means to address issues of creativity, personal transition, physical illness, and life-threatening diseases. In 1980 she co-led a workshop in Greece recreating the Eleusinian Mysteries. She was on the faculty of the Feminist Studio Workshop and founded the Writing Program at the Women's Building in Los Angeles.

KATRINA L. MIDDLETON has been published in *Enclave, Pinchpenny, Music West, Wind Chimes, Auburn Sunday Journal, Suttertown News,* and *Experiences.*

DOLORES ROSENBLUM is a social worker at Rush-Presbyterian-St. Luke's Medical Center in Chicago and is collecting the life stories of older black women. She is the author of a book on Christina Rossetti, *The Poetry of Endurance.*

KAY SCHODEK is a clinical social work supervisor at the Walter E. Fernald State School for the mentally retarded. She wrote her mastectomy poem as a member of a poetry group initiated by Alice Davis.

BETTIE SELLERS has taught at Young Harris College since 1965. She served as chairperson of the Division of Humanities, 1975–85. She was named Goolsby Professor of English, 1986. She has published several books of poetry, most recently *Liza's Monday and Other Poems* (1986) and *Satan's Playhouse* (chapbook) (1986). Poems have been published in the *Arizona Quarterly,* the *Georgia Review, Georgia Journal, Appalachian Heritage, Green River Review, An Introduction to Poetry* (a college text), and *Women in Literature* (1987).

JOANNE SELTZER has published more than two hundred poems in journals such as *Poetry Now, The Village Voice, Minnesota Review,* and *Blueline.* She is a member of the Poetry Society of America and Associated Writing Programs, and a former member of the Feminist Writers' Guild's National Steering Committee. Her biography is included in *The World Who's Who of Women, International Authors and Writers Who's Who, Personalities of America,* and other reference guides.

EMILY SIMS has been writing poetry for fifteen years. She studied with William Meredith at Connecticut College, Sonia Sanchez at Temple University, and Alexandra Grilikhes at the Philadelphia College of the Performing Arts.

PHYLLIS HOGE THOMPSON travels between Albuquerque, Silver City, and Mogollon, New Mexico. Her most recent book is *The Ghosts of Who We Were* (University of Illinois Press, 1986). She writes a weekly column about Mogollon, a ghost town with about twenty full-time residents, for the *Silver City Enterprise*. Recent work is appearing in *Hudson Review, Prairie Schooner,* the *Garden State,* and *Raccoon.*

LORRAINE VERNON has published two books of poetry, *No. 3, Frank Street* (1978) and *The Flautist of Köln* (1979). *Mastectomy, an April Journal* appeared in 1981. She is a member of the League of Canadian Poets and British Columbia Federation of Writers.